Especially for:

_____

From:

_____

Date:

_____

Published by Barbour Publishing, Inc., P.O. Box 719, Uhrichsville, Ohio 44683, www.barbourbooks.com

Our mission is to publish and distribute inspirational products offering exceptional value and biblical encouragement to the masses.

Member of the
Evangelical Christian
Publishers Association

Printed in China.

*Inspiration for the
Christmas Season*

His Name
Shall Be
Called

BARBOUR
PUBLISHING

CONTENTS

Introduction

For unto us a child is born, unto us a son is given:
and the government shall be upon his shoulder:
and his name shall be called Wonderful, Counsellor,
The mighty God, The everlasting Father,
The Prince of Peace.

ISAIAH 9:6

What better time of the year than Christmas to focus on the wonderful names of Jesus. From His place of honor beside the Father in heaven to His humblest of moments at the Nativity of His birth, Jesus Christ is our hope, our Rock, our Savior. Within these pages you'll find selections from the classic devotional *Wonderful Names of Our Wonderful Lord,* plus Christmas-themed inspiration. Spend time reminding yourself of the many names of the King of kings this holiday season and allow the truth of Christmas takes root in your heart the whole year through.

Wonderful Counselor

Wonderful

For unto us a child is born,
unto us a son is given. . .
and his name shall
be called Wonderful.
ISAIAH 9:6

*

Jesus is "the same yesterday, today, and forever,"
and men who think Him commonplace or at most
only an unusual man will sometime stand ashamed
and confounded as they hear this prophecy fulfilled,
"His name shall be called Wonderful." Today He
is working just as wonderful works as when He
created the heaven and the earth. His wondrous
grace, His wonderful omnipotence, is for His child
who needs Him and who trusts Him, even today.
Attempt great things for God and expect great
things from Him, and you will begin even now
to say, His name is Wonderful.

Resting Place

My people hath been lost sheep:
their shepherds have
caused them to go astray,
they have turned them away
on the mountains: they have
gone from mountain to hill,
they have forgotten their restingplace.

JEREMIAH 50:6

Truly there is rest for the weary, for Jesus is "Our Resting Place." Therefore, in the middle of the toil and the weariness, in the middle of the struggle and strife, let us ask that our ears may be opened to hear Him who said, "Come unto me, all ye that labour and are heavy laden, and I will give you rest" (Matthew 11:28). To abide in Him in continuous love and obedient faith is to find Him "Our Resting Place."

Christmas day is a day of joy and charity.
May God make you very rich in both.
PHILLIPS BROOKS

✳

I am not alone at all, I thought. I was
never alone at all. And that, of course,
is the message of Christmas. We are never
alone. Not when the night is darkest, the wind
coldest, the world seemingly most indifferent.
For this is still the time God chooses.
TAYLOR CALDWELL

✳

Bless us Lord, this Christmas,
with quietness of mind; Teach us
to be patient and always to be kind.
HELEN STEINER RICE

The Rose of Sharon

I am the rose of Sharon.
SONG OF SOLOMON 2:1

✦

Child of God, there is no mood of
your life where Jesus fails to fit your need,
to brighten as a brilliant rose your life.
In joy or sorrow, sunshine or shadow,
day or night, He blooms for you. Look
on Him, then, today, not only on the cross
for you, not only on the throne, but near
you, close beside your path, "The
Rose of Sharon."

O star of wonder, star of night,
Star with royal beauty bright,
Westward leading, still proceeding,
Guide us to Thy perfect light.
JOHN HENRY HOPKINS

*F*ather God, this "Wonderful, Counsellor. . .mighty God. . .everlasting Father. . .Prince of Peace" You sent to earth has been with You for all eternity. But He became human through a very specific family, the line of Israel's King David.

You had promised David—the youngest son of a man named Jesse— that his kingdom would be an everlasting one. With Jesus' birth, You brought forth a rod from the stem of Jesse, a branch out of Jesse's roots. And You began the fulfillment of yet another promise.

You tell us where Jesus came from to encourage us with where *we're* going. Amen.

Counsellor

For unto us a child is born, unto us a son is given. . .
and his name shall be called. . .Counsellor.
ISAIAH 9:6

✦

*N*ot often is He called "Counsellor" now.
Even God's saints continuously ask of men instead
of God, "How may I find God's will?" Conference
after conference is held by both the world and the
church to find by human wisdom some better plan
for earthly government, or for the church, or for
the welfare of our earthly life and walk. But how
rarely do we bow together or alone to seek that
heavenly wisdom, that divine counsel, which alone
will enable us to find our way out of the mazes
in which we wander. When will His name be
joyfully and triumphantly proclaimed as
"Counsellor" by His people? By you?

The Shepherd of Israel

And I will set up one shepherd over them. . .
and he shall be their shepherd.
EZEKIEL 34:23

Is any name of our God more comforting
to weary, needy children than Jesus' name of
Shepherd? Feeding, leading beside still water,
watching over all our wanderings, bringing us as
the Shepherd of Israel brought His flock out
of the wilderness over the Jordan into the
land of peace and plenty.

Teach us to trust in You, O Shepherd of Israel. Amen.

Lord, You're always thinking of my needs: You give me confidence in my faith when I believe in the birth of Jesus Christ.

There are always doubters, Father, and some of them say that Jesus wasn't truly human—that He was just a spirit, some kind of illusion. And if He wasn't truly human, He couldn't possibly affect our human condition.

But Jesus *did* come in the flesh—born outside a real Bethlehem inn, raised in the real town of Nazareth, ministering as an adult from the real village of Capernaum. . . and dying on a very real cross outside Jerusalem.

May I never forget, Father, that Jesus is *real*. Amen.

The Carpenter

Is not this the carpenter?
MARK 6:3

✦

The Carpenter! Two things are suggested in this
verse. Joseph is not mentioned and is probably not
living. Jesus is working at the carpenter's bench and
continued to do so until He assumed His place in His
public ministry. We can and should visualize Him in
His daily tasks—a man among men. How near He
seems to us! What a joy to know that He handled the
hammer and sharpened the saw, planed the plank,
and helped to supply the food for the family. Test this
picture of Him with any false system, and observe
the contrast. No matter what our calling may be, the
Carpenter will be one with us. We can walk arm in
arm with Him in our daily tasks.

O, Carpenter of Galilee, be our ideal always! Amen.

Born thy people to deliver,
Born a child and yet a King,
Born to reign in us forever,
Now thy gracious kingdom bring.
Charles Wesley

Lord, there are many stories of angelic visits in Your Word: an angel delivered a message to Mary, another spoke to Joseph, and a host of angels appeared to the shepherds as they were watching their sheep at night. Each of these people knew they'd had an encounter with a messenger from You.

You tell us to be hospitable to everyone, because we might host an angel without knowing it. Help me, Lord, to treat each guest in my home as if I knew they were a heavenly being sent by You. Amen.

Restorer

He restoreth my soul: he leadeth me in the
paths of righteousness for his name's sake.
PSALM 23:3

✦

We wander from God and from the paths
of righteousness—from following Him beside
the still waters—till we lose the way, lose joy,
lose the sound of His voice. Then the Master
"restoreth [the only use of this form in the Old
Testament] our soul"; "brings us back into his
way," into the paths of righteousness.

Oh gracious Restorer, bring back my wandering soul
as You would a straying sheep, and lead me on in the
paths of righteousness "for Your name's sake." Amen.

Jesus Christ the Same

Jesus Christ the same yesterday,
and to day, and for ever.

HEBREWS 13:8

"The same!" How we love this verse. The world is a sinful, restless world. Uncertainty is written everywhere in human life, but the Living Word and the written Word are unchangeable. What was He before He was born of the Virgin Mary? He was God. What was He when He lived and labored among men? He was God. What was He when He hung on the cross? He was God. What is He today? Still God, with the same pierced hands and feet, the same scarred side, the same loving heart—for having loved His own, He loves them still and will love them throughout eternity. Nothing in human thought or language is more wonderful.

Lord Jesus Christ, You are the same. Help us to
sense it and intensify our love for You and may
it also be always "the same." Amen.

Time was with most of us, when Christmas Day, encircling all our limited world like a magic ring, left nothing out for us to miss or seek; bound together all our home enjoyments, affections, and hopes; grouped everything and everyone round the Christmas fire, and made the little picture shining in our bright young eyes, complete.

CHARLES DICKENS

The Light of the Morning

And he shall be as the light of the morning,
when the sun riseth, even a morning without clouds.

2 SAMUEL 23:4

No single name or picture of our Lord could possibly reveal Him as the full supply of all our need. Our Lord is to His people not only "The Morning Star," but when the lights of night fade in dawning day, He becomes the "Light of the Morning." When all the earth has passed, when all of earth's visions fade and flee away, when the great glory of that morning of our eternal life in heaven shines on us, we will find that the One who lit all our earthly pilgrimage is still our source of life and guidance in heaven and will be to those for whom He has prepared a place the "Light of the Morning." "So shall we ever be with the Lord" (1 Thessalonians 4:17).

What I'd like to have for Christmas
I can tell you in a minute
The family all around me
And the home with laughter in it.

EDGAR A. GUEST

From home to home, and heart to heart,
from one place to another.
The warmth and joy of Christmas
brings us closer to each other.

EMILY MATTHEWS

Somehow, not only at Christmas,
but all the long year through,
The joy that you give to others,
is the joy that comes back to you.
JOHN GREENLEAF WHITTIER

I heard the bells on Christmas Day,
their old familiar carols play,
And wild and sweet the words repeat
of peace on earth, goodwill to men!
HENRY WADSWORTH LONGFELLOW

Mighty God

My Strong Rock

Bow down thine ear to me; deliver me speedily:
be thou my strong rock, for an house of defence to save me.
PSALM 31:2

✦

No sorrow of men is so deep and dark and
bitter as to be without a refuge, a rock, a safe
retreat. My soul, however deep your sorrow,
however dark your sin, however hopeless your
lot among men, the Man of Sorrows bore your
sin in His own body on the tree. He carried
all your grief. He is your "Strong Rock."
A strong, safe house, in which I am defended
from myself, the world, the devil.

Rock of ages, cleft for me,
Let me hide myself in Thee. Amen.

The King's Son

Give the king thy judgments, O God,
and thy righteousness unto the king's son.
PSALM 72:1

---

*H*ow little do our hearts discern the homage
due to God as King and to Jesus as His Son.
We bow our heads, we lift our hats, we pay our
homage to the fleeting, trifling power of earth's
great men, but do we, as we enter the house of
God, bow humbly and revere "The King's Son?"
Are earthly thoughts hushed and earthly words
stilled as we gather in the house of God, and even
when our spokesman voices our desires to Him,
do wandering thoughts of earthly things deprive
us of the blessing and the answer to our prayers?

Lord, teach us how to pray,
that we may truly worship You. Amen.

If Jesus had wanted for any weething,
A star in the sky, or a bird on the wing,
Or all of God's angels in heav'n for to
sing, He surely could have it,
'cause He was the King.

JOHN JACOB NILES

Emmanuel

Behold, a virgin. . .shall bring forth a son,
and they shall call his name Emmanuel.

MATTHEW 1:23

✦

This was the prophecy of Isaiah 7:14:
"Therefore the Lord himself shall give you a sign;
Behold, a virgin shall conceive, and bear a son,
and shall call his name Immanuel." "Emmanuel"
(God with us)! What a wonderful God and Savior
He is, and He is with us as He promised in
Matthew 28:19–20: "Go ye therefore, and teach
all nations, baptizing them in the name of the
Father, and of the Son, and of the Holy Ghost:
Teaching them to observe all things whatsoever
I have commanded you: and, lo, I am with you
always, even unto the end of the world." Let us
sense His presence and make Him real. Walk,
talk, live with, and love Him more and
more as the days go by.

Lord Jesus, we know that You dwell in us.
May we enjoy Your fellowship today. Amen.

Listen to the angel's song, all you who have a troubled heart. "I bring you good tidings of great joy!" Never let the thought cross your mind that Christ is angry with you! He did not come to condemn you. If you want to define Christ rightly, then pay heed to how the angel defines Him: namely, "A great joy!"

MARTIN LUTHER

Smiles. Small kindnesses extended.
A neighbor bringing a plate of cookies.
A piano playing Christmas carols in
a department store. Cups of wassail
offered in places of business. . .
Clerks and customers wishing each other
Merry Christmas and Happy Holidays!
Wouldn't it be wonderful if this
thoughtfulness lasted throughout the
year? Maybe it could start with me.

DEBORAH BOONE

The Christ, the Son of God

*She saith unto him, Yea, Lord: I believe
that thou art the Christ, the Son of God.*
JOHN 11:27

✳

*H*ere is a remarkable confession from the lips
of Martha, "The Christ, the Son of God."
Lazarus was in the tomb. Her eyes, no doubt,
were full of tears, her soul full of sorrow, but her
faith in Jesus as the Christ never wavered. She
heard that Jesus was coming and called Him
"Lord"; then she said, "I believe that thou art the
Christ, the Son of God." How sweet! How blessed!
But yet the heart of Jesus was pained, for He
groaned in spirit because of her lack of faith that
He would answer prayer and raise up Lazarus.

*Lord Jesus, help us never to disappoint You in our faith in
Your power and Your promise to answer our faith. Amen.*

The Lord, Mighty in Battle

Who is this King of glory? . . .
the LORD mighty in battle.
PSALM 24:8

✦

*N*o life can be lived for God in these difficult days without terrific conflict. Foes within and foes without assail each saint continuously. Principalities and powers are arrayed against the child of God who seeks to serve his Master. We have no might with which to meet "this great company that cometh against us" (2 Chronicles 20:12), but the Lord, Mighty in Battle, is our Savior, our Intercessor, our Elder Brother, our ever present Friend.

"Sure, I must fight if I would win;
increase my courage, Lord." Amen.

We hear the Christmas angels
The great glad tidings tell;
O come to us, abide with us,
Our Lord Emmanuel.

PHILLIPS BROOKS

Lord of All

The word which God sent unto the children of Israel,
preaching peace by Jesus Christ: (he is Lord of all).
ACTS 10:36

✦

Jesus Christ is Lord of all men. Peter was a Jew
and did not want to depart from Jewish ground,
but God sent him a vision from heaven to make
clear to him that He was no respecter of persons.
"While Peter yet spake these words, the Holy
Ghost fell on all them which heard the word."
Our Lord loves all; He died for all; He
commissions us to go and preach to all. The world
is the field, and every soul living has a claim on
us, which we must meet and answer for. What a
wonderful Lord of All! What a wonderful Gospel!
What a wonderful salvation!

Oh Lord of all, rebuke us today for our selfishness,
our lack of likeness to You, and fill us with the Holy
Ghost that we may gladly be witnesses to all men. Amen.

*L*ord God, during this season, we celebrate the gift of Your presence here on earth, when You arrived as a baby. But You did not remove Your presence when You returned to heaven—You promised that the Holy Spirit would come to be with us. You have not left us alone!

What a comfort in this promise. In this declaration, You have promised the rest we so desperately desire. We don't need to chase after You or compete for Your attention. You are with us continually! I can find true rest in that promise. Amen.

Good news from heaven the angels bring,
Glad tidings to the earth they sing:
To us this day a Child is given,
To crown us with the joy of heaven.
MARTIN LUTHER

41

The Savior of the World

And we have seen and do testify that the
Father sent the Son to be the Saviour of the world.
1 JOHN 4:14

A lost and ruined world, bound by the shackles
of sin, dominated by the demon Satan, helpless
and hopeless! What can be done? Only God, the
sovereign against whom the world has sinned, can
solve the question, and He has. He sent His Son.
We have seen Him by faith and testify to the truth
that He is indeed a Savior. He has saved us through
faith in His name and finished work. We *must* testify.
We *must* bear witness. Wherever we go, whatever
we do, let us tell it—"He is a world Savior."

Lord, may we be faithful witnesses to Your
saving power and tell the love story to all. Amen.

My Glory

But thou, O LORD, art a shield for me;
my glory, and the lifter up of mine head.
PSALM 3:3

That God is "glory"—or "excellence"—
beyond our understanding, none can deny.
But do our hearts look up to Him today in
humble, earnest worship, and know the truth, and
speak the truth—"You are My Glory"? Our *safety*
lies in the fact that He possesses us. Our deepest,
holiest *joy* comes only when we humbly say in
the hour of secret worship, "You are mine."

Oh Lord my Glory, be my shield this day. Amen.

The birth of the baby Jesus stands as the most significant event in all history, because it has meant the pouring into a sick world of the healing medicine of love which has transformed all manner of hearts for almost two thousand years.

GEORGE MATTHEW ADAMS

Christ Jesus

Christ Jesus came into the world to
save sinners; of whom I am chief.
1 TIMOTHY 1:15

"The Anointed Savior" came into the world
to save sinners. Where did He come from? He
came from the glory. Who was He? He was God,
the Creator. "I came forth from the Father, and
am come into the world," He says in John 16:28.
Sin separates man from God and separates God
from man. Sin is opposition to God. Mankind is
under the curse of sin and has no power to atone
(make a covering) for its sin. God alone could meet
the issue and solve the problem, and He has.
He came and bore man's sin on the cross and
paid the penalty with His own blood.

We bow in Your presence, Anointed Savior,
and pour out our souls with gratitude to You.
Help us to live close to You today. Amen.

Father, the angel told the shepherds not to be afraid, because he was bringing a *joyful* message. The message was one for the benefit of all people: a Savior had been born.

Then many angels joined together for a celebration in the skies above Bethlehem. Their praises to You inspired the shepherds to go immediately to Bethlehem to find the Baby.

Lord God, I thank You for the joy surrounding Jesus' birth. I desire to seek You with the same joy and purpose the shepherds had that night. Amen.

Jesus came!—and came for me.
Simple words! and yet expressing
Depths of holy mystery,
Depths of wondrous love and blessing.
Holy Spirit, make me see
All His coming means to me;
Take the things of Christ, I pray,
Show them to my heart today.

FRANCES RIDLEY HAVERGAL

Eternal Father

The Everlasting Father

For unto us a child is born, unto us a son is given. . .
and his name shall be called. . .The everlasting Father.
ISAIAH 9:6

✦

Who has not mourned a father's death and
felt the loss of his transient power and helpfulness?
The Child who was born in Bethlehem, who
gave His life for you, is not only your Savior and
your King, but "His name shall be called The
Everlasting Father." In His everlasting love, within
His everlasting arms, within His Father heart
which pities you—His child—you will find
safety, rest, and comfort.

My Firstborn

Also I will make him my firstborn,
higher than the kings of the earth.
PSALM 89:27

Loose thy shoe from off thy foot; for the place
whereon thou standest is holy" (Joshua 5:15). The
Eternal Father, God, is speaking. "My Firstborn
I will make higher than the kings of earth."
Oh, you who are the last-born of the Father, the
Firstborn is your Elder Brother. You have shared
His humiliation to your salvation. You will share
His exaltation to your eternal glory.

We worship You, Lord Jesus, God's Firstborn! Amen.

Father God, I thank You for considering us Your children. We recognize that we are indeed Your children—our full reliance is on You, our Father. We feed on Your Word. You protect us. You discipline us when we lose our way. You are always ready to help us when we call.

I thank You that You forgive me unconditionally when I sin against You. Help me to extend that same forgiveness to others who offend me. May Your name be glorified in the unity of Your children. We long for the day when we're with You. Amen.

His Only Begotten Son

*For God so loved the world, that he gave his only
begotten Son, that whosoever believeth in him
should not perish, but have everlasting life.*

JOHN 3:16

✦

*H*ere is the most beloved verse in the
Bible. What a revelation of God, of Christ,
of the depths and power of love! How
could He? Abraham gave his son, and God
graciously gave him back. But *God's Son*—
the Son of His love—the Only Begotten
One—was given to a lost world, to sinful
men. How did He give Him? Clothed in
human form—a man! Oh, the wonders of
such a love! How it should stir our hearts!
How we should love God for His gift! How
we should love our Lord Jesus Christ—
God's Only Begotten Son!

*Let us with throbbing hearts for a lost world
go out today, and all the days, to tell the
story to sinful, suffering men. Amen.*

*H*eavenly Father, this is the time of year when families and friends gather for meals together. There is usually an abundance of food, and the time sharing fellowship is so special. We have so many happy memories of those times spent around a table.

Help me to remember those who may *not* have friends or family to share a meal with. May I focus on those poor or disadvantaged this year. Lead me to someone I can invite to a special meal. Amen.

The Christmas message is that there is hope for a ruined humanity—hope of pardon, hope of peace with God, hope of glory— because at the Father's will Jesus Christ became poor and was born in a stable so that thirty years later He might hang on a cross.

J. I. PACKER

The Sent of the Father

As thou hast sent me into the world,
even so have I also sent them into the world.
JOHN 17:18

✦

From the glory which He had with the Father before the world was, He was sent into this world of sin and shame to redeem sinful men. He was God's Apostle—God's "Sent One." His prayer now to the Father is that they might be *sanctified* (set apart) as He was set apart for the work of redemption. He prays that His disciples might also be set apart for the great work of saving men. Christ has not changed. This prayer was for us, also, as He says in verse 20: "Neither pray I for these alone, but for them also which shall believe on me through their word." His holy desire is that we might be in the world with the same message that He Himself had.

Lord Jesus, help us to recognize today Your
call and our calling to save souls. Amen.

His Own Son

He that spared not his own Son, but delivered him up for us all, how shall he not with him also freely give us all things?

ROMANS 8:32

✦

"His Own Son," "His Only Son," "The Son of His Love"—the dearest, the best He gave out of His great heart freely, lovingly, once for all to the sinful children of men. Having given us His best, will He withhold anything from us? Why do we doubt Him? Why do we live such poor, selfish, sordid lives, when the world is so needy, when hearts are so heavy and broken? Why do we fail to take hold of what He has so freely offered us? Is there not a challenge to us here? Let us meet it today.

Lord, help us to believe and with joyful hearts ask for great things for a needy world in the name of Your Son. Amen.

*L*ord, during this time of year, many will exchange gifts with friends and family. But as special as those gifts might be, when our life here on earth is over, not one of us will take them with us.

We thank You for the food and clothing You provide for us—the daily blessing for our daily needs. Help us to be thankful for what we have, and not to worry about accumulating more. We ask for godliness, so that we can be truly content. Amen.

The Way

Jesus saith unto him, I am the way.
JOHN 14:6

He is the Way—"a Way without deviation"—
the straight and narrow Way, the only Way
which leads directly to the Father. There are
a thousand ways which lead to destruction, to
eternal darkness and separation from the Father.
Satan has multiplied agents pointing to his wicked
way, but Christ is the signpost, saying: "This is the
Way; walk ye in it." When we walk in *the Way* we
walk in the light. We journey with Him in sweet
fellowship. What a joyful journey! The Way is
lightened by His countenance. He holds us by the
hand. He supplies our needs. What a Savior!

*Lord, help us to keep in touch with You as
we travel along the heavenly highway to
the home prepared for us by You. Amen.*

We all need wisdom. . .
Wisdom to choose the right
paths to take in life. . .
Wisdom to know right from wrong. . .
Wisdom to see what truly matters most.
The wise men were willing
to give up their homes,
Their familiar habits,
And travel far to seek wisdom. . . .
It takes courage to set out
looking for something new.
But if we make this journey,
God will shine His light into our lives,
Like the glimmer of that long-ago star.
All we have to do is follow.

ELLYN SANNA WITH VIOLA RUELKE GOMMER

Lord, I have tried to prepare my household for this holiday season. I have purchased the "extras" I need on hand.

You tell me to not withhold good when it's in my power to give. You say not to tell neighbors to come back later if they need to borrow something now. Sometimes I want to hold onto those things, just in case *I* may need them. But if I put myself in their place, I would appreciate the assistance.

May I not dwell on the "giving up" but rather on the "helping out"—and do as You have commanded. Amen.

His Dear Son

Who hath delivered us from the power of darkness, and hath translated us into the kingdom of his dear Son.

COLOSSIANS 1:13

To "his dear Son" is here attributed the deliverance and translation of the believer from the power of Satan, the ruler of this dark world. Ignorant of Him, millions are dwelling today, controlled by the power of a Satanic nature, resisting His Word, and doomed to eternal darkness. There is only One who can deliver men. It is His Dear Son. We are the possessors of this truth and have experienced it. How can we, how dare we, be indifferent to the blinded souls all around us when His Dear Son is longing to have them respond to His call "Come unto Me"?

*Oh beloved Son, make us light-bearers
to darkened souls today. Amen.*

Eternal Life

This is the true God, and eternal life.
1 JOHN 5:20

✦

Jesus is "the True God," and He is "Eternal Life"
also. Human life is eternal, for it must be lived here
or in another world. It must be spent in the heart of
God our Savior or in the abode of Satan. "Where
will you spend eternity?" is one of the most solemn
questions ever asked of men. The only answer is
found in God's Word, and it is answered there a
hundred times and in a hundred ways. To believers,
eternity means life with God our Savior, and
we look forward with joyful anticipation; but
to the unsaved, it is a fearful prospect.

*Lord, help us in dealing with people to
be truthful and loving as we paint the
pictures of a future without a Savior. Amen.*

Unto us a Child is born!
Ne'er has earth beheld a morn,
Among all the morns of time,
Half so glorious in its prime!

Unto us a Son is given!
He has come from God's own heaven,
Bringing with Him, from above,
Holy peace and holy love.
HORATIUS BONAR

The Son of the Father

*Grace be with you, mercy, and peace, from God
the Father, and from the Lord Jesus Christ,
the Son of the Father, in truth and love.*

2 JOHN 1:3

✦

*H*ere is a threefold blessing bestowed by John:
"Grace, mercy, and peace from the Son of the
Father." This is the testimony of the Father: "This
is my beloved Son, in whom I am well pleased"
(Matthew 17:5), and He is the *only begotten* of the
Father. There is no separation between Father and
Son. There is a union which is unspeakable. "He
that hath seen me hath seen the Father" (John
14:9). "I and my Father are one" (John 10:30).
The blessing is to be bestowed in "truth and love."
Truth without love may be cold, hard, harsh. Love
without truth may be purely sentimental, but,
when combined, they truly represent the message
of "the Son of the Father," for the Son
is the truth, manifested in love.

*We pray, our Father, that this benediction of grace,
mercy, and peace may rest on us today as we
meditate on "the Son of the Father." Amen.*

*L*ord, we praise You for the gift of Your Son. He died for all people, without discrimination, to give us a life free of condemnation. Because of Your love, we are now forgiven—and can look forward to eternal life with You.

We did nothing to bring about Your love, nor could we ever do anything to deserve it. All the glory belongs to You alone. We praise You and thank You for the gift You freely and willingly gave. Amen.

May Emmanuel find
welcome in our hearts,
Take flesh in our lives,
And be for all peoples
the welcome advent
Of redemption and grace.
THE ROMAN MISSAL

Prince of Peace

The Prince of Peace

For unto us a child is born, unto us a son is given. . .
and his name shall be called. . .The Prince of Peace.
ISAIAH 9:6

He who proclaimed to loyal hearts, "Peace I leave with you, my peace I give unto you: not as the world giveth, give I unto you" (John 14:27), is rightly called "The Prince of Peace." He who brought such peace to earth was rejected of men and waits still to be crowned on earth; but He gives before that royal day a peace that surpasses understanding to every trusting heart. Have you received it? Will you, in loyalty to "The Prince of Peace," accept in humble faith His peace today?

A Sign

This child is set. . .for a sign
which shall be spoken against.
LUKE 2:34

Our Lord Jesus Christ was a significant sign
to Israel. The prophecies had long before
made clear that Israel was to be tested when
the Messiah came. Some would believe and
follow Him. Some would reject and crucify Him.
Our Lord gave testimony to this fact when Pilate
asked Him, "Art thou a King?" And His answer
was: "To this end was I born, and for this cause
came I into the world" (John 18:37). Poor Pilate,
he had his evidence but would not accept it.
Where is he? The Sign has been given to our land,
also. Where are the multitudes? The same old
story will be told again and again.

Oh Lord, have compassion upon this
poor land. Inspire Your servants to be brave
and true in sounding the alarm. Amen.

May the spirit of
Christmas bring you peace,
The gladness of
Christmas give you hope,
The warmth of
Christmas grant you love.

UNKNOWN

The Prince of Life

And killed the Prince of life, whom God hath raised from the dead; whereof we are witnesses.

ACTS 3:15

"The Prince of Life"—a remarkable title to give to our Lord when viewed in contrast with Barabbas, the murderer who took life. One—the bestower of life; the other—the destroyer of life. He came that men might have life and life more abundantly. How many there are who ignore and reject Him, who will never have the joy of living and reigning with Him through the eternal ages. Are we doing our best to make Him known to lost men?

Lord Jesus, Prince of Life, stir our hearts with compassion for the lost, and help us today to make You known to a blinded soul. Amen.

There's more, much more, to Christmas
Than candlelight and cheer;
It's the spirit of sweet friendship
That brightens all year.

It's thoughtfulness and kindness,
It's hope reborn again,
For peace, for understanding,
And for goodwill to men!

UNKNOWN

Come Thou long expected Jesus, born to set
Thy people free. . .let us find our rest in Thee.

CHARLES WESLEY

He has come! the Prince of Peace. . .
come to scatter with His light all
the darkness of our night.
HORATIUS BONAR

Come, old men and grey, the star leads
the way. . . . Filled with His grace,
depart ye, God's servants, in peace.
G. A. STUDDERT KENNEDY

Jesus knocks at the door of our hearts,
and when we open, He fills us with His joy.
CORRIE TEN BOOM

A Prince and a Savior

Him hath God exalted with his right
hand to be a Prince and a Saviour.
ACTS 5:31

Here is a picture and a theme for our meditation. A convict—a criminal in the sight of men— hanging on a tree, dying an awful death of shame, suffering the agonies of hell itself that the question of sinful man's sin might be settled forever—exalted by God to the highest heights—a Prince! But to establish His title He became the sin-bearer that He might become the sin-blotter. Destined to deepest depths of human suffering and humility, but raised to the highest heights of honor and glory. Oh, the wretchedness of our sin which demanded it, and the wonders of a Savior which delivered it!

Lord Jesus, our Prince and our Savior, we yield
ourselves to You with glad hearts. Amen.

Christ

Blessed be the God and Father of our
Lord Jesus Christ, who hath blessed us with
all spiritual blessings in heavenly places in Christ.
EPHESIANS 1:3

Three times is the word "bless" used in this verse. God is a blessed God, and He showers His blessings on His people. What are the spiritual blessings in Christ? They are spiritual gifts, the blessing of the Gospel—the "Good News" from God. They include the eternal purpose and precious promises of God which are to be manifested in the present, in the future, and throughout eternity. As you read your Bible, note them. How many! How strengthening! How encouraging! How satisfying! How enduring! And all *in* Christ and *only* in Him.

How we rejoice, oh Christ of God, that by faith we are
in You and all of Your blessings are for us. Help us to
appropriate them with thankful hearts. Amen.

He has come! the Christ of God;
Left for us His glad abode,
Stooping from His throne of bliss,
To this darksome wilderness. . . .

He has come! the Prince of Peace;
Come to bid our sorrows cease;
Come to scatter with His light
All the darkness of our night.

HORATIUS BONAR

The Prince of Princes

He shall also stand up against the Prince of princes;
but he shall be broken without hand.

DANIEL 8:25

*B*y every word which men could understand
Almighty God has sought to exalt His Son, so that
in all things He might have the preeminence in
our lives, as King of kings, as Lord of lords, and
as in this text, "The Prince of princes." In earthly
kingdoms it is very often true that on the prince
who is heir apparent to the throne is lavished
more affection than on the king himself. What
about our love and affection to "The Prince of
princes"? Although sitting now at the right hand
of the Father and one with Him, He is waiting
to be crowned on earth. Do we pay Him more
devotion and deeper love than we do to these
erring mortals who reign over us? Let us, in the
real things of daily life, exalt Him to His rightful
place and pour out our devotion to Him.

*H*eavenly Father, at times it takes *effort* to rest in You. Especially at this time of year, I look at others around me who seem to get whatever they want—and I have to admit that it sometimes bothers me. And then there are those who seem to succeed even when living contrary to Your ways.

Lord, please quiet my mind when I compare what seems to be the success or wealth of others with my lack of it. I want to choose to rest in You, to wait patiently, and not to fret. Only then will I have true success. Amen.

*When we celebrate Christmas,
we are celebrating that amazing time
when the Word that shouted all the
galaxies into being, limited all power,
and for the love of us came to us in the
powerless body of a human baby.*
MADELEINE L'ENGLE

Jesus Christ

Grace be unto you, and peace, from him which is, and which was, and which is to come; and from the seven Spirits which are before his throne; and from Jesus Christ, who is the faithful witness, and the first begotten of the dead, and the prince of the kings of the earth.

REVELATION 1:4–5

*H*ere is a fourfold adoration of our Lord. Four titles are given to Him, the first of which is "Jesus Christ" (the Anointed Savior). "How sweet the name of Jesus sounds to a believer's ear." He is, He was, and He is to come! That completes the vision of Himself. The "seven spirits before the throne" represent the sevenfold operation of the Lord throughout the earth. We must join with the heavenly host and sing his praises.

Oh Anointed Savior, help us to unite with all the heavenly host in glorifying Your name. Amen.

The Prince of Kings of the Earth

Jesus Christ, who is the. . .
prince of the kings of the earth.
REVELATION 1:5

A glorious title! Sometime in the future there will be a gathering of all the hosts that have ever lived on this earth, and of the hosts of heaven, and in their presence will stand *One* who will be proclaimed "Prince of the kings of the earth— King of kings and Lord of lords!" The kingdoms of the world are His by right and title, and before Him all must bow. He is Lord of all who exercise authority and King of all who reign. He has not yet asserted His authoritative rights. They are still in abeyance, but the day is coming when every scepter will be broken and every crown laid at His feet.

We praise You, Lord of Hosts, our Savior;
we will be with You then. Help us to do
our best to hurry the glad day. Amen.

$\mathcal{L}$ord, You told us not to lay up treasures for ourselves on earth, but rather in heaven. You don't oppose possessions on earth, but You want us to keep them in perspective.

The wise men brought You gifts of gold, frankincense, and myrrh. Those treasures were meant as a gift for the one they journeyed a great distance to see. Yet the true treasure was the first gift they gave—their worship, when they fell before You.

Help me to keep the right perspective, focusing on the treasures that will last forever. Amen.

Jesus Christ Our Lord

That as sin hath reigned unto death,
even so might grace reign through righteousness
unto eternal life by Jesus Christ our Lord.
ROMANS 5:21

✳

*H*ere we have the grouping of three titles,
"Jesus" (Savior) "Christ" (Anointed) "Lord"
(Master). In a few words the great problem of
the ages is solved. Sin, with its death-dealing
power, wore the crown of victory over mortal
man, but there was One greater than Satan, the
author of sin, and in that One was manifested the
victorious power of grace (unmerited favor) by
which, through the sacrifice of Jesus Christ,
God's condescending love could be manifested
in His Son, our Lord and Master.

"Jesus Christ, our Lord"—we breathe the words
with joyful lips and give You thanks for that grace
which has saved and which keeps us. Amen.

Are you willing to believe that love is the strongest thing in the world—stronger than hate, stronger than evil, stronger than death—and that the blessed life which began in Bethlehem nineteen hundred years ago is the image and brightness of the Eternal Love? Then you can keep Christmas.

HENRY VAN DYKE

$\mathcal{L}$ord, Your peace will reign in the one who keeps his mind fixed on You. That promise can settle anxious thoughts and times of doubt.

When Mary was told she would give birth to Jesus, anxiety and doubt could have overtaken her. But even though it was difficult for her to understand, she expressed only faith. Mary believed her experience would be just as the heavenly messenger had described.

Lord, help me to keep my mind on You, so that I—like Mary—may experience Your perfect peace. Amen.

****

Christ the Savior

****

The Christ

Thou art the Christ,
the Son of the living God.
MATTHEW 16:16

---

*T*his is the title of the long-looked-for Savior—
the Anointed One. Prophets had foretold His
coming, and now His kingly authority is recorded.
Over three hundred times is this title used in the
New Testament. From "Christ" comes the word
"Christian," and from "Christian" comes the
word "Christianity." Today this land of ours is
the foremost Christian nation of the world.
Our gospel is the Gospel of Christ of which
we are not ashamed, for it is the power of God
unto salvation to everyone that believes.

Lord, as "Christ-ones" let us honor You by
having the same anointing power resting on
us as we enter the service of the day. Amen.

Horn of Salvation

And hath raised up an horn of salvation
for us in the house of his servant David.
LUKE 1:69

✦

*H*ere is a title which suggests the strength
and power of our Lord—"Horn of Salvation."
The word *horn* as used in the scripture signifies
"strength" and is often found in Hebrew literature.
In the horns, the bull manifests his strength.
The Lord Jesus Christ is our strength and a very
present help in time of trouble (Psalms 118:14;
28:7; 37:39). "But the salvation of the righteous
is of the LORD: he is their strength in the time of
trouble" (Psalm 37:39). You may be tempted and
tried today. You may have burdens to bear.
Let Him be your "Horn of Salvation."

Lord, strengthen us by the power of
Your might for today's service for You. Amen.

Our Savior, the Dayspring from on high, has visited us, and we who were in darkness and shadows have found truth!

BYZANTINE PRAYER

A Man of Sorrows

He is despised and rejected of men; a man of sorrows, and acquainted with grief: and we hid as it were our faces from him; he was despised, and we esteemed him not.

ISAIAH 53:3

He who was the source of all joy, the giver of all peace, He before whom angels and archangels bow in adoration, is also called a "Man of Sorrows." Grief broke His heart, crushed out His life. Will we through disobedience, rebellion, or lack of love or service, or worship, add to the sorrows which He bore; or will we murmur if we, too, will be permitted to partake of His sorrows, or to share His grief? He sorrowed all alone, except perhaps as angels ministered to Him in Gethsemane's deep shadow. But He shares your grief; He carries all your sorrow and comforts those who trust in Him. Will we not worship and adore the Man of Sorrows?

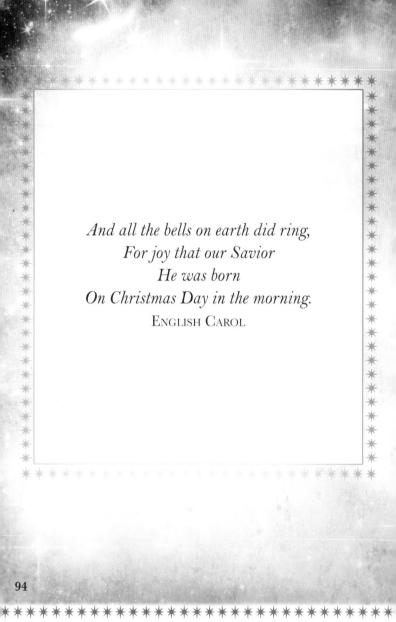

And all the bells on earth did ring,
For joy that our Savior
He was born
On Christmas Day in the morning.
ENGLISH CAROL

Father, why would You send Your own Son to live among sinful people, ultimately dying a cruel death on the cross?

This verse answers our questions: You allowed Jesus to die to break the power of the devil. Satan thought he'd defeated You, but Jesus' Resurrection proved that He was not in any way bound by death. And with the eternal life Jesus offers, neither are we!

Thank You, Lord, for sending Jesus to earth. Born in humble circumstances in the tiny, insignificant village of Bethlehem, Jesus lived a perfect life, died a sacrificial death, and purchased my salvation with His blood.

I need never fear death. Jesus has defeated it! Amen.

The Servant of Jehovah

Behold my servant, whom I have chosen.
MATTHEW 12:18

✦

*J*esus, the prophesied Servant! Isaiah had portrayed Him. Jehovah had chosen Him. All of God's ways were known to Him from the beginning. You hear the echo of His voice, "I delight to do thy will, O my God!" Nothing was too great for Him to do, for He was the Creator, and nothing was too hard for Him, for He had all power. Nothing was too small for Him to do, for He stooped to notice a widow's mite and give a mighty lesson from it. What a gracious privilege to be yoked with Him in service.

*Dear Lord, let us labor with You, the "Servant of Jehovah,"
today and thus make it a good day for You. Amen.*

Messiah

The woman saith unto him, I know that
Messias cometh, which is called Christ:
when he is come, he will tell us all things.
JOHN 4:25

There is no book like the Bible, and there never can be. Christ's interview with the woman at the well and His revelation of Himself is unique and contrary to any conception that could have been made of Him. The Samaritans, as did the Jews, anticipated a Christ (an Anointed One). This was the promise given in Deuteronomy 18:18. This woman was the last one we would have chosen for such a revelation—but her soul was filled at once with the Spirit of life and hope, and her lips bore a testimony—humiliating to herself—but bringing salvation to a multitude. Oh, that our lips might bear such convincing, convicting, and converting testimony.

Lord, make us like this Samaritan woman! Amen.

Joy to the earth, the Savior reigns!
Let men their songs employ;
While fields and floods,
rocks, hills, and plains,
Repeat the sounding joy.
ISAAC WATTS

Jesus the Christ

Then charged he his disciples that they should tell no man that he was Jesus the Christ.
MATTHEW 16:20

✦

This title, "Jesus the Christ," is used a hundred times in the New Testament. "The Savior—the Anointed One"—a combination that magnifies the office of the One whom we long to worship. The time had not yet come for them to preach the story of redemption. They were to hold their peace for a season, but He tells *us* to go into all the world and tell to all people the wonderful message of Jesus Christ and His finished work. Are we obeying the command?

Dear Father, as we go out today with this precious name in our hearts and on our lips, help us to tell someone of the wonders of the man, Your Son, Jesus the Christ! Amen.

*F*ather God, You made a promise through the prophet Isaiah—a promise You fulfilled seven hundred years later with the birth of Your Son, Jesus Christ.

Only You could make a virgin conceive a child. Only You could offer salvation through that child. Only You would step into Your creation as a human being—*Immanuel* means "God with us"— and experience the life we live on this earth.

I thank You, Father, for the promise of a child—the virgin's Son who would later die on the cross for my sins. Amen.

*F*ather God, I am so thankful that You came to earth to die for my sins. You arrived as a baby, then spent Your life preparing to take the sins of the world onto Yourself on the cross. Your blood has covered my sins.

What freedom I enjoy in Your forgiveness! Yet what a sacrifice You made to bring about that freedom. You suffered physical pain, You were mocked, and Your friends betrayed You. But You did it all as a gift for me, because of Your love. Thank You, Lord, for the blessing of forgiveness. Amen.

A Ransom

The Son of man came. . .to give his life a ransom for many.
MARK 10:45

"A ransom for many!" Here Christ is identified as the penalty paid for the sins of the world. As sinners under the judgment wrath of God, He took our place and paid the penalty and the price of our deliverance with His own blood. Listen to the drops of blood as they fall from hands and feet and wounded side! They voice the words, "The ransom price for *my* sins and for the sins of the whole world." Oh, that men everywhere would believe it and receive it! How dear, how precious is He to us, washed clean in His blood and freed forever from the punishment due to us.

Lord, may our ransomed souls well up
in praise to Your glorious name! Amen.

One Son, His Well-Beloved

Having yet therefore one son, his wellbeloved, he sent him also last unto them, saying, They will reverence my son.
MARK 12:6

✦

$\mathcal{T}$he Savior is in Jerusalem. The chief priests and scribes come to Him and question His authority. Jesus answers them in the parable of the vineyard, picturing to them the treatment of the servants who were sent to gather the fruit, telling the story—so old, so strange—of the attitude of the human heart toward God. He sent His Son, His Well-Beloved Son, and they took Him and killed Him and cast Him out. How could they? They have cast Him out of the schools and many of the churches, though all we have of earthly civilization and comforts today we owe to Him.

God's Well-Beloved Son, we enthrone You today in our hearts. Help us to worship and adore You. Amen.

May you have the gladness
of Christmas, which is Hope;
The spirit of Christmas, which is Peace;
The heart of Christmas, which is Love.

AVA V. HENDRICKS

The Lamb of God

The next day John seeth Jesus coming unto him,
and saith, Behold the Lamb of God,
which taketh away the sin of the world.

JOHN 1:29

✦

*H*ow shall we say in a few words what springs up
in our hearts and would break out from our lips?
"The Lamb which taketh away our sin" is a better
rendering, for He takes it away by *bearing* it. He
bore the sins of those who received Him while here
on the earth, and He bore them *away* when He
paid the penalty on the cross and shed His atoning
blood. *God's* Lamb! No one else could be God's
Lamb. He was the *voluntary* offering. What can we
do? Believe it, accept it, take our place with Him.

Let us look on You every day—Jesus, Lamb of God—
counting nothing too good to give to You
or too much to do for You. Amen.

*Like the shepherds who heard
the angels' wonderful tidings, we, too,
can forget the night we see around us.
We know the day has dawned.
If you commit yourself to this belief, those
around you may be as startled and disbelieving
as those who heard the shepherds' news.
But why walk in the darkness anymore when
the Christmas star shines bright as day?*

ELLYN SANNA

Sometimes the glad tidings of Christmas
seem simply too good to be true. But. . .
as you keep quiet and listen, you will
know deep down in your heart that you
are loved. As the air around about you,
so is His love around you. Trust that
love. . . . It will never fail.
AMY CARMICHAEL

The Son

My Beloved Son

This is my beloved Son, in whom
I am well pleased; hear ye him.
MATTHEW 17:5

✳

*W*onderful manifestation! A cloud of glory
overshadowing what was too deep for human eyes
to penetrate. The voice of Jehovah attesting that
Jesus was His beloved Son and that His words
were to be heard. The same voice and the same
message were heard in chapter 3, verse 17 when
our Lord was baptized, and once again in John
12:28 in Jerusalem. "*His* beloved" and *our* beloved!
How marvelous is that testimony to Him whom
we have learned to love, and because we love
Him, we are beloved of the Father.

Lord, may we breathe it over and over again today,
"I am my beloved's and my beloved is mine." Amen.

The Son of Mary

Is not this. . .the son of Mary?
MARK 6:3

$\mathcal{T}$he Carpenter, the "Son of Mary," has come back to His hometown from an evangelistic trip in which He had worked many miracles. The people were astonished at His teaching. Prejudice possessed them. "Is not this the son of Mary?" We never worship Mary as our Catholic friends do, but we do honor her above all women—God's chosen vessel to bear His Son and fulfill His prophecy. How true He was to the last. See Him on the cross, and hear His last words to Mary, from John 19:26, "Woman, behold thy son" (John, the beloved, to whom He had said, "Behold thy mother").

Blessed title—Son of Mary! The Babe who is one day to rule the world and at whose feet we will bow in worshipful adoration! Let us do so now. Amen.

*On the morning of Christ's nativity. . .
the Son of Heav'n's eternal King. . .
our great redemption from above did bring.*

JOHN MILTON

Thou Son of the Most High God

And cried with a loud voice, and said, What have I to do with thee, Jesus, thou Son of the most high God?
MARK 5:7

Here we are confronted with another testimony from an unclean spirit—"Son of the most high God," he calls Jesus. What unseen powers compelled this significant title? Was it brought about by being face-to-face with Himself? Judas betrayed Him, but this poor, demon possessed man worshipped Him. In these strange days many teachers, professors, and preachers refuse to honor Him as *the Son*, but only as *a Son* of God. But we lift our hearts to Him and say,

"Son of the most high God, be our companion this day and may we withhold nothing from You." Amen.

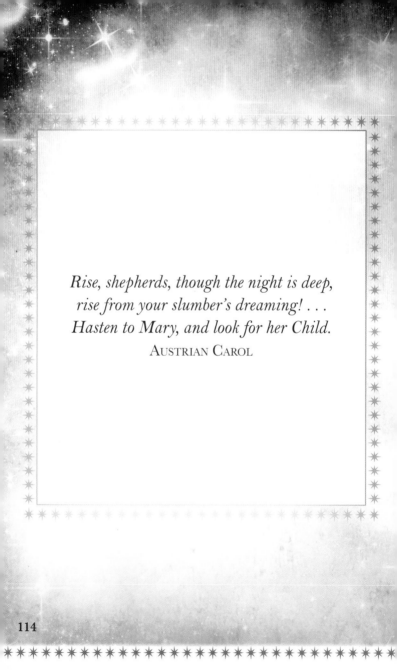

Rise, shepherds, though the night is deep,
rise from your slumber's dreaming! . . .
Hasten to Mary, and look for her Child.

AUSTRIAN CAROL

$\mathcal{F}$ather, You had promised in Isaiah's time that You would send a son, a child to be born to a virgin. And centuries later, to a young Jewish virgin named Mary, You sent an angel with this promise: "Behold, thou shalt conceive in thy womb, and bring forth a son, and shalt call his name JESUS."

Lord, Your word is true, no matter how many years may pass. Your promises can always be relied on. Your predictions always come true.

Thank You, Father, for the baby boy You conceived in Mary's womb—the Son named Jesus who would save His people from their sins.

The Son of David

The book of the generation of
Jesus Christ, the son of David. . .
MATTHEW 1:1

✦

*O*ur Lord was a lineal descendant of David, the king. This entitled Him to the right of sovereignty over David's land, and when He was here among men, we are told, there was no other claimant to the throne of David. Herod sought to destroy the Child-King Jesus, but Egypt was chosen as a refuge place for Him. The heart of Herod was like the hearts of all the children of men who will not have Him to rule over them. He was bearing us on His heart, as a child, for He is the same "yesterday, today, and forever," and He is our refuge now.

Jesus Christ, Son of David, may our hearts be
linked up with Your great heart always. Amen.

Son of Abraham

The book of the generation of
Jesus Christ. . .the son of Abraham. . .
MATTHEW 1:1

$\mathscr{T}$hree titles in one verse, "Jesus Christ—Son of David—Son of Abraham." Abraham was the head of the covenant nation. God had given to him the promise that in his seed should all the nations of the earth be blessed. Jesus submitted to the Jewish law in righteousness. He lived as a Jew, and He preached to the Jews. He died for the Jews as well as for all people. "So then they which be of faith are blessed with faithful Abraham" (Galatians 3:9). How wonderful! God manifested in the flesh as Abraham's seed and yet the One who made the promise to Abraham!

Oh promised Son of Abraham and Son of God,
our Savior, hold us fast in faith in Your Word. Amen.

The second person in God, the Son, became human Himself: was born into the world as an actual man—a real man of a particular height, with hair of a particular color, speaking a particular language. . .the eternal being, who knows everything and who created the whole universe, became not only a man but (before that) a baby. . . . The Son of God became a man to enable men to become sons of God.

C. S. LEWIS

Son of Man

The Son of man shall be delivered unto the chief priests,
and unto the scribes; and they shall condemn him to death.
MARK 10:33

✦

𝓘n the ninth chapter Jesus had said, "The Son of man is delivered into the hands of men, and they shall kill him." How earnestly He sought to stress the fact of His approaching sacrifice upon His disciples, and how He longed for their sympathy; but, alas, how hard is the human heart! How difficult it is for Him to win us to Himself! "The Son of man must suffer many things" (Mark 8:31), He had said, but the saddest of all was the failure of His own beloved disciples to enter into the burden He bore as He approached the cross.

Oh Holy Son of Man, give to us the loving hearts that will enter into fellowship with You in all things. Amen.

Father, this is the time of year when people make their "wish lists." Discussions turn to what will be "under the tree" on Christmas morning. Covetousness can run rampant.

Please, Lord, I pray that You will guard my tongue in my conversations. May I only speak positive, kind, contented words. Guard my heart, too, that I do not give covetousness a place there.

I thank You that You are always with me and will never leave me. May my actions prove that I believe Your Holy Spirit dwells within me. Amen.

When He sent us His Son,
God crossed the distance that once
separated human beings from Him.
Our King came to live with us.
No wonder Christmas is a day of joy!
ELLYN SANNA

Christ, the Son of the Blessed

Art thou the Christ, the Son of the Blessed?
MARK 14:61

---

*T*he court is convened. The high priest is presiding. Charges had been brought against the Lord Jesus Christ by false witnesses, but they had not agreed. The high priest put to Him a question: "Art thou the Christ, the Son of the Blessed?" And He answered, "I am." There was no denial of the title, but a straight confession of His Sonship, heirship, power, and coming glory. And when He comes—if He delays still a season—we will be among those who will be caught up in the clouds to meet Him in the air and with the hosts of heaven praise Him "Blessed!"

Lord, Jesus Christ, Son of the Blessed,
hurry the glad day. Amen.

The Son of the Highest

He shall be great, and shall be
called the Son of the Highest.
LUKE 1:32

✦

*T*his is the message of the angel to Mary, and
here is a remarkable coincidence. In Mark 5:7,
we have the evil spirit in the man in the tombs
giving a similar title to Jesus, "Son of the most
high God." The title given Him here is in
fulfillment of Psalm 132:11: "The LORD hath
sworn in truth unto David; he will not turn from
it; of the fruit of thy body will I set upon thy
throne." David's heir is to reign as Son of the
Most High God, and that time only waits for
the completion of the church which is His body.
Let us do our best each day to win souls for
Him and thus hurry the day when we will
be with Him and reign with Him.

Son of the Highest, we bow to You, we worship You.
Help us to magnify Your name today. Amen.

✳ ✳ ✳ ✳ ✳ ✳ ✳ ✳ ✳ ✳ ✳ ✳ ✳ ✳ ✳ ✳ ✳ ✳ →

Jesus Christ the Lord

✳ ✳ ✳ ✳ ✳ ✳ ✳ ✳ ✳ ✳ ✳ ✳ ✳ ✳ ✳ ✳ ✳ ✳ →

Jesus Christ

The book of the generation of Jesus Christ. . .
MATTHEW 1:1

✳

*H*ere is the first title given to our Lord in the New Testament—Jesus Christ. Matthew 1 contains a host of names, covering three periods of fourteen generations each, but *one* name stands out like a radiant star to light all the others; *one person* to whom all must render allegiance—Jesus (Savior) Christ (the Anointed One). At His feet every knee will bow in heaven and on earth.

Let us pour out our hearts to Him in praise and in prayer this day and every day. Amen.

A Nazarene

And he came and dwelt in a city called Nazareth:
that it might be fulfilled which was spoken by
the prophets, He shall be called a Nazarene.
MATTHEW 2:23

Nazareth was a town in the northern border
of the plain of Esdraelon. Here came the angel
Gabriel and announced to Mary the coming birth
of Christ: "And the angel came in unto her, and
said, Hail, thou that art highly favoured, the Lord
is with thee: blessed art thou among women"
(Luke 1:28). On the night of His betrayal our
Lord asked the question, "Whom seek ye?"
They replied, "Jesus of Nazareth," and He
said, "I am He" (see John 18:4–5).

Jesus of Nazareth, may we never be ashamed
to be called the followers of the lowly Nazarene.

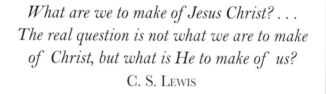

What are we to make of Jesus Christ? . . .
The real question is not what we are to make
of Christ, but what is He to make of us?
C. S. Lewis

A Branch out of His Roots

And there shall come forth a rod out of the stem of Jesse,
and a Branch shall grow out of his roots.

ISAIAH 11:1

---

*O*f all the miracles that attest to the deity of our
Lord, including the miraculous preservation of the
scriptures, none is more wonderful or convincing
to the honest, faithful heart than the preservation,
not only of Israel, but of that section of Israel,
humble in its origin, which revealed our Lord to
be born of the family of David and of Jesse. Out
of the nations scattered over the earth, out of the
line of kings who long had ceased to reign, there
came, as the prophet said, a "Branch out of His
roots" of the stem of Jesse. And He who was of
the seed of David will just as surely come again
to reign once more over Israel, and through
Israel, over all the earth.

Lord, our faint hearts believe once more in
God's eternal truth and faithfulness. Amen.

All poor men and humble,
All lame men who stumble
Come haste ye, nor feel ye afraid;

For Jesus, our treasure
With love past all measure,
In lowly poor manger was laid.
OLD WELSH CAROL

The day and the spirit of Christmas rearrange the world parade. As the world arranges it, usually there come first in importance—leading the parade with a big blare of a band—the Big Shots. . . . Then at the tail end, as of little importance, trudge the weary, the poor, the lame, the halt, and the blind. . . . But in the Christmas spirit, the procession is turned around. Those at the tail end are put first in the arrangement of the Child of Christmas.

HALFORD E. LUCCOCK

Jesus

Thou shalt call his name JESUS:
for he shall save his people from their sins.
MATTHEW 1:21

✦

Over seven hundred times in the New Testament
is this name used—"Jesus" (Joshua). How familiar
we are with that name! Joshua of the Old
Testament saved Israel by leading them through
the River Jordan, fought their battles, and was
steadfast in his allegiance to God and His people.
He was a type of our Lord who is our Joshua;
who fights our battles for us; who is our leader,
our protector, our Savior! Who will never cease
His lordship until He has us safely in the fold on
the other side. Hallelujah, what a Savior!

This day, Savior of our souls, in whom we
are set apart for eternity, guide us by Your
Holy Spirit to the praise of Your grace. Amen.

Jesus of Nazareth

And I answered, Who art thou, Lord? And he said unto me,
I am Jesus of Nazareth, whom thou persecutest.
ACTS 22:8

✦

*M*ore than twenty times in the scriptures our Lord is called "Jesus of Nazareth." Here it is remarkable. Paul is telling the story of his conversion. He is bound with chains, a prisoner in the hands of the Roman authorities. He says that the words which came to him from the heavens were "Saul, Saul, why persecutest thou me?" And in answer to his question "Who art thou, Lord?" came the answer, "I am Jesus of Nazareth." That is His name *now*. From the glory He acknowledges His earthly title—"Jesus of Nazareth." Jesus is God. He made the worlds, but He acknowledges the little obscure town of Nazareth, His hometown on earth.

Jesus of Nazareth, we want to be one with You.
Guide us to Your glory. Amen.

*Increasingly I rejoiced in the gospel—
the amazing good news—that the
Creator of what to us human beings
is this bewildering and unimaginably
vast universe, so loved the world that
He gave His only Son, that whosoever
believes in Him should not perish, but
have everlasting life. . . . Everlasting
life, I came to see, is not just continued
existence but a growing knowledge—
not merely intellectual but wondering
through trust, love, and fellowship—
of Him who alone is truly God, and
Jesus Christ whom He has sent.*

KENNETH SCOTT LATOURETTE

The Prophet of Nazareth

This is Jesus the prophet of Nazareth of Galilee.
MATTHEW 21:11

This great demonstration had been planned by God and foretold by Him (Zechariah 9:9). Our Lord comes into Jerusalem riding upon the foal of a donkey. The crowd is vast; the enthusiasm is great. "Who is this?" is the cry; and the answer is, "This is Jesus, The Prophet of Nazareth." A despised Nazarene! A prophet from an obscure village! We are all proud if, by chance, we were born in some noted place; but God, when He took the form of a man, was born in a manger and made His home in Nazareth. For our sakes He became poor that we through His poverty might be made rich.

Let us meditate on the riches of His grace, bow at His feet and kiss them as we adore Him; and may we walk humbly today with the despised Nazarene. Amen.

$\mathcal{L}$ord, You have adopted me—You chose me! I was a sinner, yet You loved me enough to send Your Son to die as a sacrifice for me. I can't comprehend how painful that must have been for You. You were separated from Your Son, even turning away as He took on the pain and sin of all mankind.

But you endured all that so I could call You *Abba*—"Daddy." You replace my fear with a heart full of love for You, Father! Amen.

*With our minds on life's looming problems
. . .we sometime forget to notice that God's
presence has crept quietly and sweetly into
the smallest details of our lives—like the
sun on our face, a warm hand in ours,
a child's laughter, and a family's love.
This Christmas season, may you see the
Christmas Baby at the heart of your life.*

ELLYN SANNA WITH

VIOLA RUELKE GOMMER

Christ, the Lord

*For unto you is born this day in the city of
David a Saviour, which is Christ the Lord.*
LUKE 2:11

✳

The heavens are opened now, and the message
of the angel of the Lord is announced—"good
tidings of great joy." The message was to the humble shepherds, and it will mean much to us if we
can, in humility of heart, take our place with the
shepherds, acknowledge our unworthiness, and
take hold of the truth in our own souls—"Unto
you is born. . .a Saviour, which is Christ the Lord"
(the Anointed One—the ruler). We are no longer
to rule ourselves. He is to rule us.

*Lord, with joy we submit our wills and surrender all to You.
Help us to magnify You this day. Amen.*

The Lord Jesus Christ

To the saints and faithful brethren in Christ
which are at Colosse: Grace be unto you, and peace,
from God our Father and the Lord Jesus Christ.

COLOSSIANS 1:2

Master! Savior! Anointed! Here, as in many
other places in the epistles, we have a combination
of names. "Grace and peace from God the Father
and the Lord Jesus Christ." They are One.
Mystery of mysteries! Hundreds of names and
titles are given to Him, but after all, He has said,
"I and my Father are one. He that hath seen me
hath seen the Father." When he descends from
heaven we will see Him in whom all these titles are
vested. Grace has its fountain in Him, and always
in every emergency and under every condition
and circumstance, His grace will be sufficient.

Gracious Lord Jesus Christ, manifest
Your grace unto us today. Amen.

Happy, happy Christmas, that can win us back to the delusions of our childhood days, recall to the old man the pleasures of his youth, and transport the traveler back to his own fireside and quiet home!

CHARLES DICKENS

The Man Christ Jesus

For there is one God, and one mediator
between God and men, the man Christ Jesus.
1 TIMOTHY 2:5

We have considered Christ as mediator and now we have the emphasis on Christ, our mediator, as the *Man* Christ Jesus. In these days when He is being demeaned by so many who are robbing Him of His deity, we should rejoice in the privilege offered us of magnifying Him as both man and God. "Great is the mystery of godliness: God was manifest in the flesh" (1 Timothy 3:16). No picture in the Bible is so marvelously thrilling, so calculated to convince and convert, as that of God dying for men. Hold Him in your thoughts, and see Him today—arms outstretched above a bloodstained body, saying, "Come unto me. . . I will give you rest" (Matthew 11:28).

Oh crucified, risen God-Man, we adore You.
Guide us today in our worship and work for You. Amen.

The Christ Child

The Young Child

*When they had heard the king, they departed; and, lo,
the star, which they saw in the east, went before them,
till it came and stood over where the young child was.*

MATTHEW 2:9

A star in the East led the wise men to a Star
that outshines all the stars of heaven. Look at this
Young Child! Fix your gaze upon His face, lying
there, His eyes looking into your own inquiring
eyes. Visualize, if you can, God manifested in
the flesh for you. God—the Young Child! The
Creator of all things! Before whom are thirty
years of human life in which He will toil with
His fellow men. Mystery of mysteries!

*Oh wonderful One, as we bow before You
today, help us to discern something of Your
devotion for the sons of men. Amen.*

The Babe

Ye shall find the babe wrapped in
swaddling clothes, lying in a manger.
LUKE 2:12

✳

*A*gain the voice of the angel rings out to the
shepherds: "Christ the Lord—The Babe—lying in
a manger." How easy it would be for the shepherds
to find Him. No other newly born babe would be
found "lying in a manger"—just One—and He,
the altogether lovely One, the foremost among
ten thousand! Sometimes the saints magnify their
human birthright and place of birth, but He was
to be a blessing to the humblest. Would not the
cattle—could they have sensed the significance of
the event—have bent their knees in homage to the
Babe? How sad to know that millions in our land
have not yet bowed their knees to Him.

Lord, may we who have named Your name bow in
humblest submission to You today and pour out our
hearts in joyful praise to You, Babe of Bethlehem. Amen.

And is it true? And is it true,
This most tremendous tale of all,
Seen in a stained glass window's hue,
A Baby in an in ox's stall?
The Maker of the stars and sea
Became a Child on earth for me?

SIR JOHN BETJEMAN

The Child Jesus

The child Jesus tarried behind in Jerusalem.
LUKE 2:43

Here we have our first view of Jesus as a young boy, interested in the business of His heavenly Father. Hear Him when Joseph and Mary seek Him: "Wist ye not that I must be about my Father's business?" (Luke 2:49) The strangeness of the story of His life is a constant surprise. God manifested in the flesh—a child—with words of wisdom falling from His lips—a message for us all, "Occupy (do business) till I come." Every disciple is a businessman or woman, and our business is the most important in all the world. Let us take as a motto for our daily life the words of the Child Jesus, "I must be about my Father's business."

Lord, help us to be busy about
Your business today. Amen.

Christmas in Bethlehem. The ancient dream: a cold, clear night made brilliant by a glorious star, the smell of incense, shepherds and wise men falling to their knees in adoration of the sweet baby, the incarnation of perfect love.

LUCINDA FRANKS

Ah, dearest Jesus, holy Child,
Make Thee a bed, soft, undefiled,
Within my heart, that it may be
A quiet chamber kept for Thee.

MARTIN LUTHER

A Star

I shall see him, but not now: I shall behold him,
but not nigh: there shall come a Star out of Jacob.

NUMBERS 24:17

✦

*W*hat could be more beautiful or more fitting
than God calling our Lord "a Star"? Those who
know Him best may say, "One day I will see him,
but not now. I will behold him, but not from
here." Far beyond our world of trouble and care
and change, He shines with undimmed light, a
radiant, guiding Star to all who will follow Him—
a morning Star, promise of a better day.

A Bundle of Myrrh

A bundle of myrrh is my well-beloved unto me.
SONG OF SOLOMON 1:13

Oh child of sorrow, Church of Smyrna, sad soul suffocating in earth's dark vapors, your Lord is for you an exquisite perfume, "A Bundle of Myrrh." A missionary, wearily walking a winding pathway in the night, suddenly came to a spot where the air was heavy with the perfume of wild jasmine and was comforted and refreshed by a fragrance preserved from non-appreciative wild animals and wilder men for a sorrowing toiler. So is your Lord to you "A Bundle of Myrrh."

The Child

For before the child shall know to refuse the evil,
and choose the good, the land that thou abhorrest
shall be forsaken of both her kings.

ISAIAH 7:16

The first, last, and foremost mark of Christ's deity was His great humility. The greatest sage and seer of all the ages, "A Child"! The Everlasting God, hoary-white with eternal years, "A Child"! Then will *we* hesitate to "become as little children," knowing that only childlike will we enter the kingdom?

The Holy Child Jesus

For of a truth against thy holy child Jesus, whom thou hast anointed, both Herod, and Pontius Pilate, with the Gentiles, and the people of Israel, were gathered together.
ACTS 4:27

𝒫eter and John are before the Council to be examined in connection with the miracle of the healing of the lame man. They gave their testimony to the fact that it was in the despised name of Jesus Christ of Nazareth that this had been done. The Council could do nothing but let them go. They went at once to the place where the church as gathered together and reported what had been done, and the assembly lifted their voices in thanksgiving, glorifying the name of the Holy Child Jesus against whom His enemies were gathered. They prayed that in the name of this Holy Child Jesus signs and wonders might be worked, and they were.

Lord Jesus, we thank You that miracles are being worked today and will be until You come again. Amen.

Heaven in earth, and God
in man. Great little One!
Whose all-embracing birth lifts
earth to heaven, stoops heav'n to earth!
RICHARD CRASHAW

The Offspring of David

I am the root and the offspring of David,
and the bright and morning star.

REVELATION 22:16

---

*C*hrist is the stem, which sprang from the root of Jesse, and He is the Offspring of David. God, the Son, created the heavens and the earth and all that are therein, yet He is the Offspring of David, David's Lord, and David's Son. He was *born* King of the Jews and *died* King of the Jews and some day He will *reign* King of the Jews. This was God's promise, and all of God's promises will be fulfilled. As the Divine Creator, He is the root of David's house; as man, He is the Offspring. He sends His angel to give this testimony to us and to the world. There is no contradiction in God's Word concerning God's Son.

We glorify Your Word and Your work, our Lord.
We look into Your face and adore You. Amen.

When candles light
December night
And Christmas joy unfolds,
Bright dreams abound
As peace surrounds
The gifts this season holds.

So gather 'round
And hear the sound
Of singing 'round the earth
The heavens ring
When we all sing
Proclaiming Jesus' birth.

Unknown

Christated was born in the first century, yet He belongs to all centuries. He was born a Jew, yet He belongs to all races. He was born in Bethlehem, yet He belongs to all countries.

GEORGE W. TRUETT

The Son

And we have seen and do testify that the Father
sent the Son to be the Saviour of the world.
1 JOHN 4:14

The apostle John is making full proof of his ministry. He is testifying to the truth from his own personal experience, conscious that he is indwelt by the Spirit and has the new nature. He says that the Son was sent for one specific purpose—to be the Savior of men, lost men. The business of the believer is to testify to that fact. The greatest business in the world is to follow in the footsteps of men like John, the fisher of men. It is not a question of church membership or of worldly possessions, but of knowledge of Him. Have you seen Him? Do you know Him? Then go and testify of Him.

Son of God, Savior of lost men, send us
out with Your love message today. Amen.

A Lamb without Blemish or Spot

But with the precious blood of Christ, as of a lamb without blemish and without spot.

1 Peter 1:19

Our familiarity with scriptural terms often causes us to minimize their meaning. Here we have two words so marvelously wonderful that we are hesitant in our effort to make any comment— "blood" and "lamb." How precious the blood! Millions and millions of drops were poured out through the ages from Abel to Christ and every one of them said: "The Lamb is not yet. But He will come. We are the testimony of His coming." And finally the spotless, pure Lamb of God finished the work of redemption. Is He precious to us? So precious that we would be willing to die in His behalf? If so, let us say to Him,

Oh Lamb of God, my Savior, purchased by Your precious blood, I surrender all to You now. Amen.